I Can Read About™
REPTILES

Written by David Cutts • Illustrated by John D. Dawson

Consultant: Dr. Edmund D. Brodie, Jr., Professor and Head, Department of Biology, Utah State University

Troll

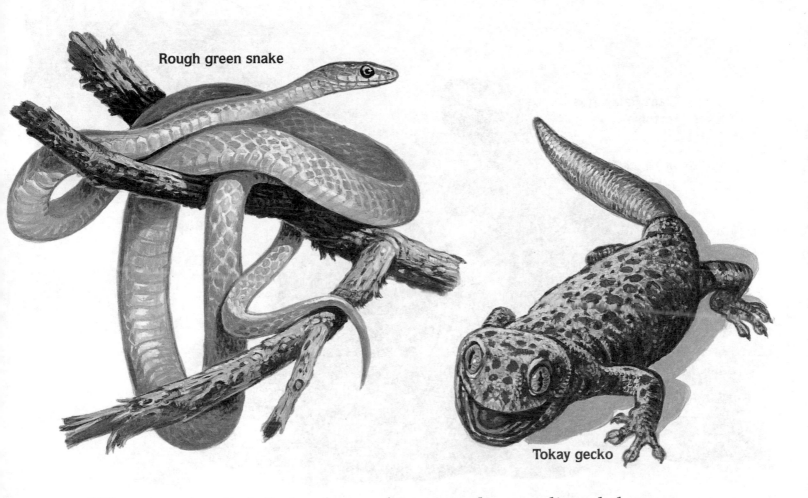

Rough green snake

Tokay gecko

What is a reptile? Is it a long, skinny snake or a lizard that can grow a new tail?

5

Giant Galapagos
tortoise

River cooter

Is it a tiny turtle in a pond or a giant tortoise that lives on land?

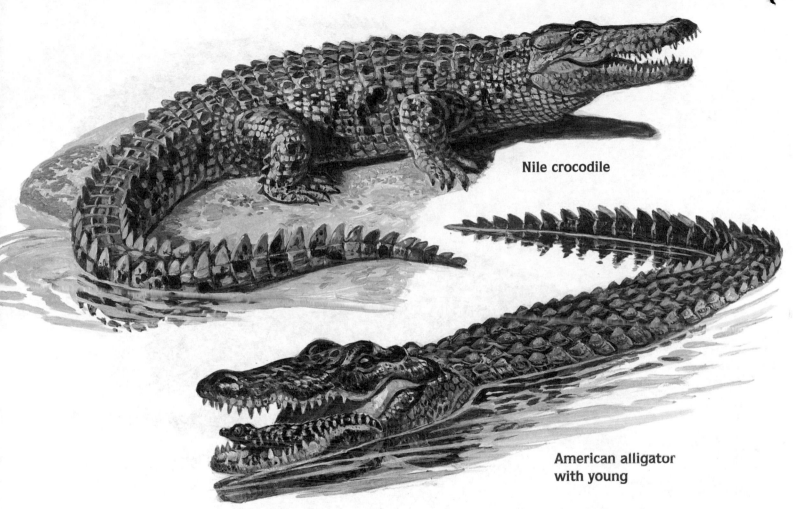

Nile crocodile

American alligator
with young

Could it be a crocodile with sharp teeth and a powerful tail or an
alligator carrying its baby to the water?

Tuatara

Elginia

Is it an animal that looks like a small dragon? Or is it a strange prehistoric creature that lived millions of years ago?

Indigo snake

Map turtle

Common iguana

Young
crocodile

All these creatures are reptiles because they are alike in certain ways. Do you know how they are alike?

9

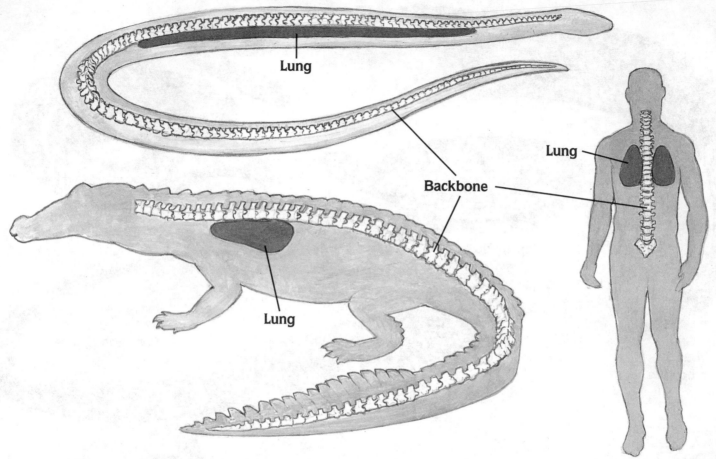

All reptiles have backbones. They also have lungs to breathe air.
You have a backbone and lungs, too. But you are not a reptile!
A reptile is different from you in many ways.

Snake scales

Lizard hide

Alligator hide

For example, a reptile's skin is very different from yours. All reptiles are covered with scales or bony plates.

Reptiles are different from you in another way. They are cold-blooded. This means a reptile's temperature goes up in warm weather and goes down in cold weather. If the weather gets too hot or cold, many reptiles go underground to escape the extreme temperatures. Some reptiles hide in the shade when it is too hot in the sun. You are warm-blooded. Your body temperature stays about the same no matter if it's hot or cold outside.

Western rattlesnake

Bradysaurus

Prehistoric reptile eggs

A few reptiles are born live from their mothers' bodies, but most are hatched from eggs. And most baby reptiles must take care of themselves as soon as they are born. Their mothers do not stay with them to feed and to protect them as they grow.

Many prehistoric animals were reptiles. And most of these reptiles, whether big or small, were hatched from eggs. These eggs had tough, leathery shells.

Such shells were a very important development for the reptiles. Before that time, creatures born from eggs had to begin life in the water because their eggs were soft and needed to be kept moist. The reptile's egg with its harder shell protected the baby growing inside. These eggs did not have to be kept moist. This meant that reptiles could lay their eggs on dry land. When the eggs hatched, baby reptiles could begin life away from the water. They were able to live in many more places on Earth than other creatures could.

Modern-day reptile eggs

Crocodile

Hognose snake

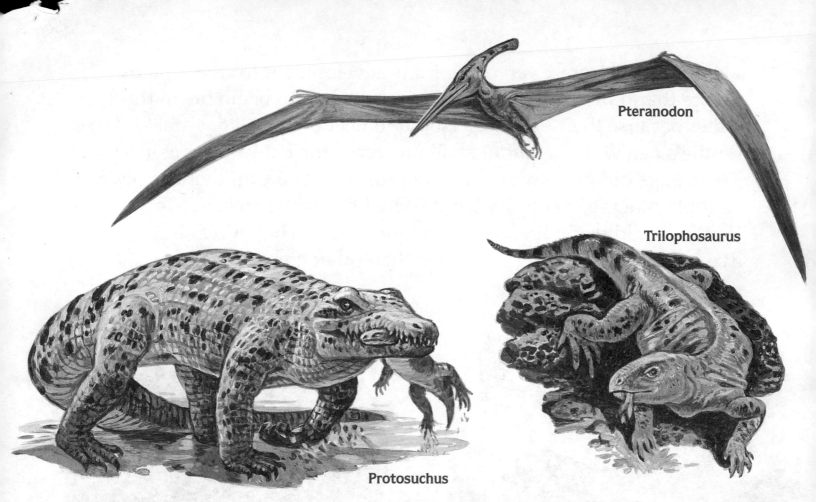

Pteranodon

Trilophosaurus

Protosuchus

Some prehistoric reptiles ate plants. Others were meat-eaters. Some lived on land, some swam in prehistoric seas, and yet others were creatures that flew.

14

Most kinds of prehistoric reptiles died out long ago. They became extinct. But certain reptiles, such as turtles, survived. Their modern relatives still live today.

Modern-day turtle

Proganochelys,
a prehistoric tortoise

Whiptail lizard

Tuatara

Rattlesnake

Crocodile

Spotted turtle

Four groups of animals make up today's reptiles. One group includes all the snakes and lizards. The three other groups are the turtles, the crocodilians, and the tuatara (too-ah-TAR-ah).

Tuatara

Scientists call the tuatara a "living fossil" because it hasn't changed in millions of years. This reptile has a row of large, sharp scales down its neck and back, which makes it look like a fierce dragon. This unusual reptile survives only on a few islands near New Zealand.

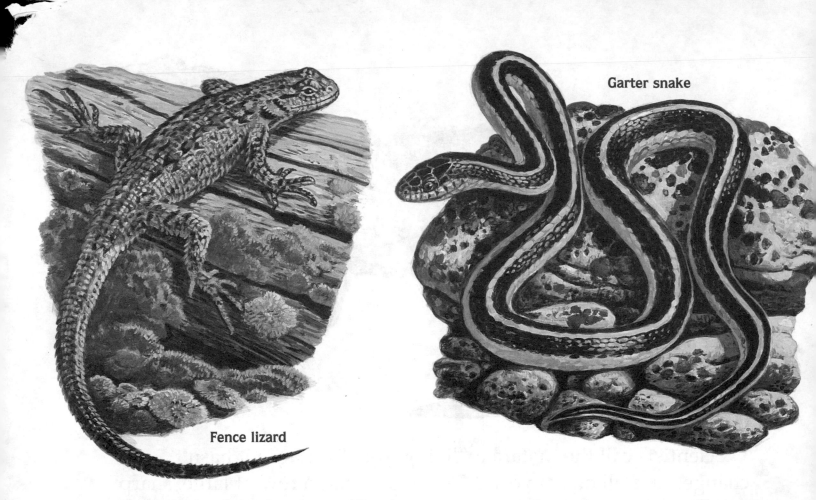

Fence lizard

Garter snake

Lizards and snakes are alike in many ways, but you can usually tell them apart. Most lizards have four legs, and snakes have no legs at all.

Slender glass snake
(a lizard)

But a few lizards, such as one called the glass snake, don't have legs. So the glass snake is not a snake after all!

The best way to tell lizards from snakes is by their eyes. Most lizards have eyelids that open and close. Snakes have no eyelids. Their eyes stay open all the time. Another difference between the two is that most lizards have ear openings. Snakes do not.

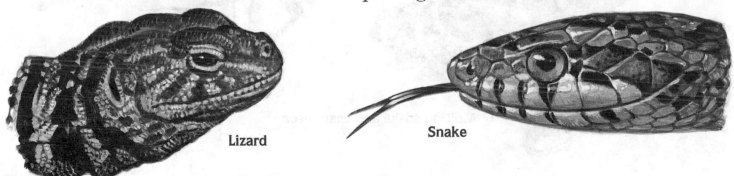

Lizard

Snake

Snakes and lizards have dry skin covered with scales. Several times a year, they grow a new skin, and the old skin dries up and comes off. This is called molting.

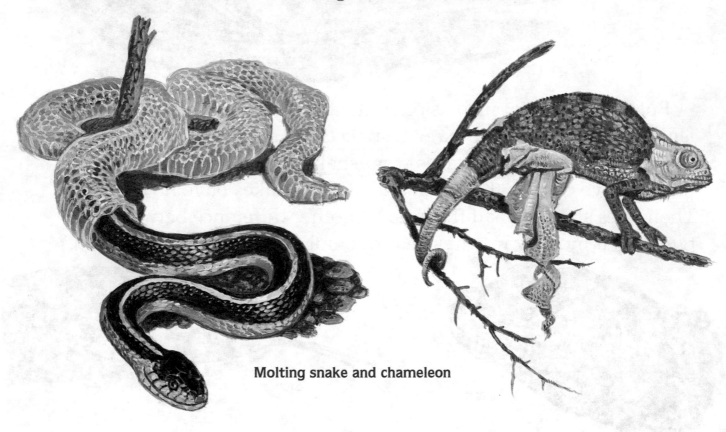

Molting snake and chameleon

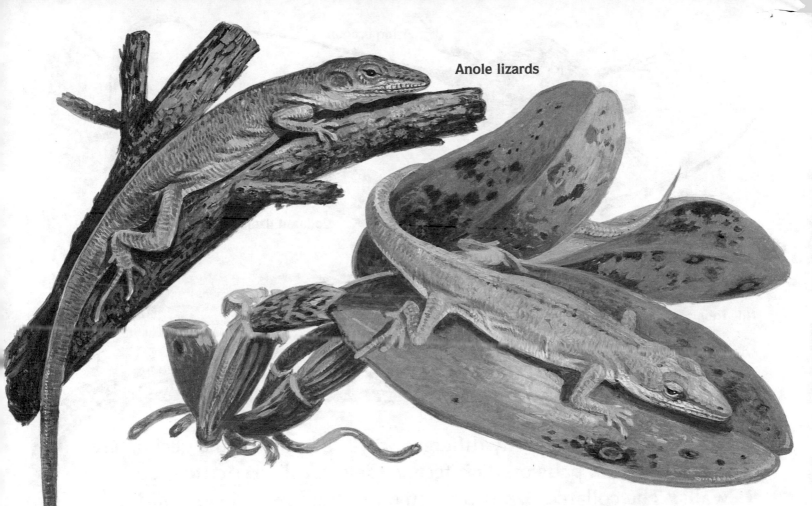

Anole lizards

    Some lizards can change colors. The chameleon's skin color changes to match its surroundings. There is also an American lizard, called thc anole lizard, that can change from bright green to brown.

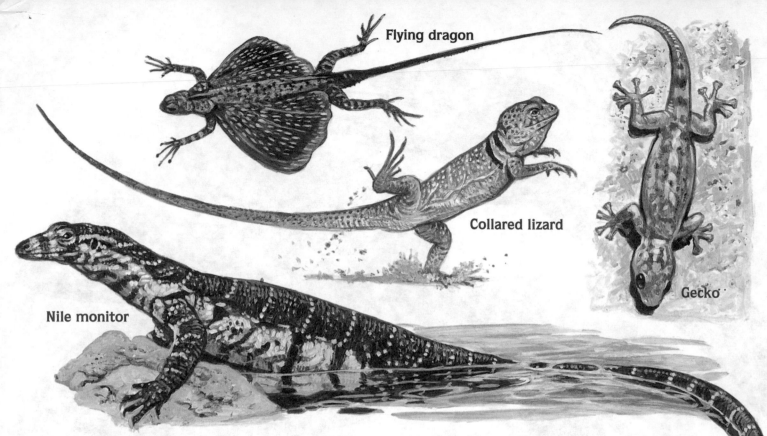

Flying dragon

Collared lizard

Gecko

Nile monitor

Lizards move in many different ways. Some, like the gecko, have special suction pads on their feet so they can climb up trees and walls. The collared lizard can run on its hind legs. One lizard is called the "flying dragon." It glides through the air by using flaps of skin that look like wings. The Nile monitor is a lizard that has many ways of traveling. It can run, swim, dig, and climb trees.

Rhinoceros iguana

Komodo dragon

Most lizards don't grow very big, but there are some exceptions. The rhinoceros iguana is more than 4 feet (1.3 meters) long. And the Komodo dragon can grow to be 10 feet (3.1 meters) long and to weigh hundreds of pounds.

Western
skink

Here's a strange trick that some kinds of lizards play on their enemies. When one of these lizards is caught by the tail, the lizard just breaks off its tail and runs away. The predator is left struggling with the still-wiggling tail.

Later, the lizard grows a new tail. Sometimes the old tail breaks off on one side, but not on the other. Then, when a new tail grows in, the lizard has two tails.

Mexican beaded
lizard

Gila monster

Only two kinds of lizards are venomous. They are the Mexican beaded lizard and the Gila (HEE-la) monster. The Gila monster lives in the southwestern deserts of the United States. This lizard's venom is strong enough to kill small animals.

Chameleon

Iguana

Lizards eat all kinds of things. Some eat insects they find on trees or catch in the air with their long, sticky tongues. Other lizards eat vegetables, leaves, and fruit.

Scarlet kingsnake

Snakes eat mice, toads, insects, and sometimes even lizards. Snakes must swallow their prey whole. Some snakes eat eggs. How can they do it? They open their mouths very wide, swallow the whole egg, and then spit out the empty shell.

Egg-eating snake

Many snakes kill animals by coiling around them and squeezing until the animal can't breathe. Such snakes are called constrictors. The longest snake in the world—the python—is a constrictor. Pythons can grow to more than 30 feet (9.1 meters) long.

Reticulated python

Venomous snakes kill their prey by biting it. The poison comes out of their long hollow teeth, called fangs.

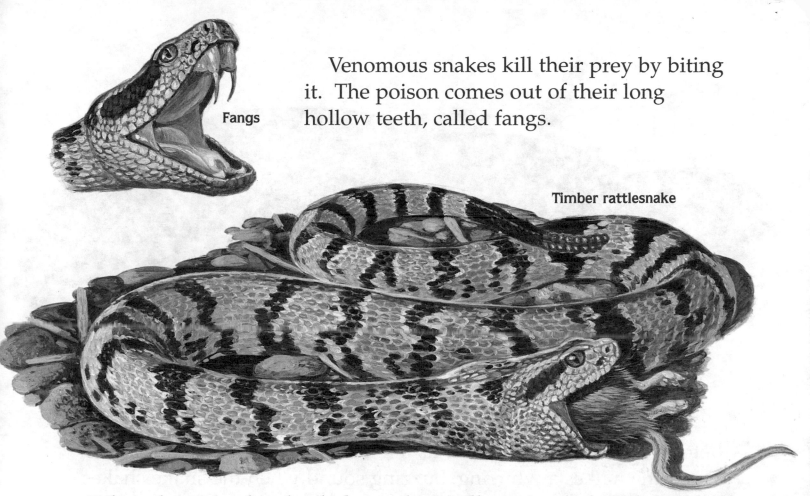

Fangs

Timber rattlesnake

When the animal is dead, the snake swallows it whole. The snake can digest everything except feathers and fur. After eating a large meal, a snake may not need to eat again for several weeks.

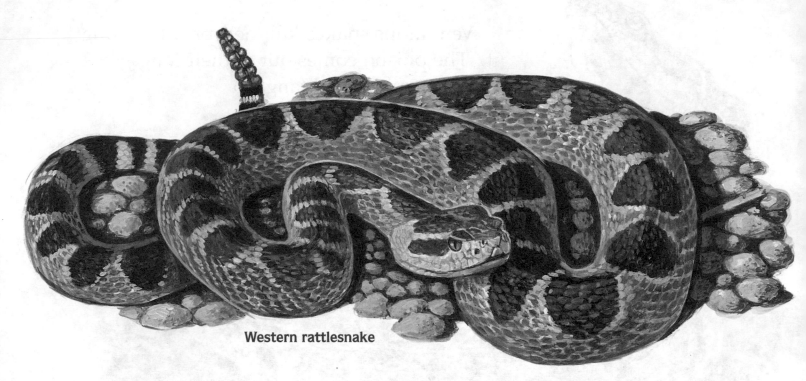

Western rattlesnake

The rattlesnake is venomous, but this animal may give a warning before it bites. On the end of its tail is a rattle made of dead scales. The rattle makes a whirring, buzzing sound when the snake shakes it. Each time the rattlesnake grows a new skin, its rattle gets a little longer. But sometimes the tip of the rattle breaks off—so you can't always tell how old a rattlesnake is by the length of its rattle!

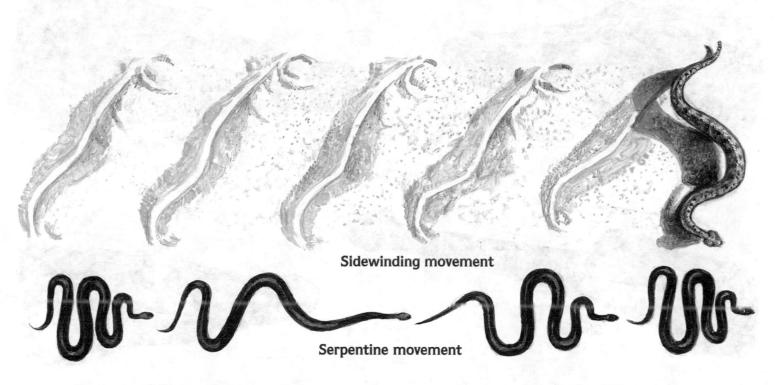

Sidewinding movement

Serpentine movement

Even without legs and feet, snakes can move very fast. The sidewinder rattlesnake moves along in a funny, sideways motion. This helps the snake get across sand.

Some snakes move by pushing against grass and pebbles.

Other snakes coil themselves up, push their heads forward, and then pull the rest of their bodies along.

Alligator

Crocodile

Gharial

Caiman

Four different creatures belong to the crocodilian family. They are the crocodile, with a long narrow head; the alligator, with a stubby, rounded head; the caiman, with a broad snout; and the gharial (GUHR-ee-ull), with a very skinny head.

All of these animals live in swampy areas near rivers. They have long tails and short, stubby legs. In the water, they tuck their legs under them and swish their heavy tails back and forth to swim.

Λ crocodile has rough, bony plates on its back. When floating in the water, a crocodile looks just like an old log. Because the crocodile's eyes and nose are high up on its head, it can see and breathe while the rest of its body is hidden in the water.

Water chevrotain

Crocodile

When a crocodile sees a small animal on the bank of the river, the crocodile swims up to its victim slowly and quietly. Then it grabs its prey in its huge jaws, pulls it into the water, and kills it.

But the crocodile can't chew its food, so to help it digest, this reptile swallows rocks! They bump and bump in the crocodile's stomach, working to grind up the food.

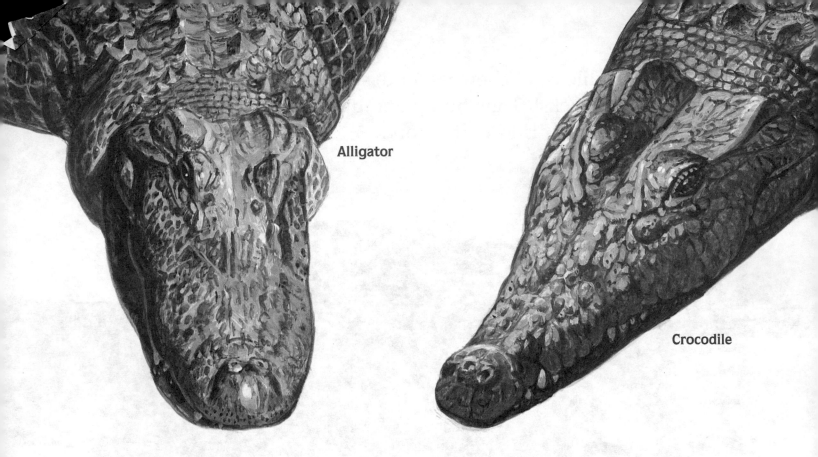

Alligator

Crocodile

    Alligators look very much like crocodiles, but there are some ways to tell them apart. The easiest way is to look at the animals' snouts. The American alligator's snout is much broader than the skinny, pointed snout of the American crocodile. Alligators are also less active than crocodiles. They often lie all day in the warm sun.

Alligator nest

Alligators are different from many other reptiles. A great number of reptiles do not take care of their young. But the mother alligator stays near her nest of eggs, guarding it from predators. After the babies hatch, she keeps them safe for about a year.

Gharial

The gharial lives in Asia. Its head may be very skinny, but this animal's jaws are strong, and its teeth are sharp. This reptile likes to eat fish.

Caiman

The caiman is a strong swimmer. As a baby, the caiman eats insects. As an adult, this reptile eats mammals, other reptiles, fish, and birds. Caimans are found in Central and South America.

Turtles are reptiles, too. They are the only kind of reptile that has a shell. The turtle's shell protects it.

Turtles that live on land are called tortoises. Others live in ponds and streams and are called freshwater turtles. Sea turtles live in the ocean.

Yellow-bellied turtle

Gopher tortoise

Hawksbill turtle (a sea turtle)

Leatherback turtle

    Sea turtles have flippers instead of legs. The leatherback turtle is covered with a tough, leatherlike skin on its back instead of a hard shell. Leatherback turtles can weigh 1,500 pounds (.7 metric ton). They are the heaviest reptiles in the world.

Although they live in the ocean, sea turtles lay their eggs on shore.

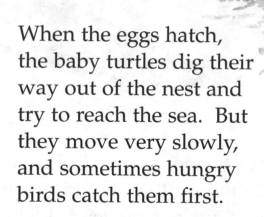

When the eggs hatch, the baby turtles dig their way out of the nest and try to reach the sea. But they move very slowly, and sometimes hungry birds catch them first.

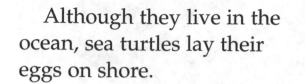

Redbelly turtle

Spotted turtle

Freshwater turtles have webbed feet. Some have pretty designs on their shells. These turtles eat insects, leaves, and small fish.

A turtle has no teeth. It uses the sharp edges of its jaws to bite and chew food.

Giant Galapagos tortoise

Land turtles, the tortoises, move very, very slowly on short, stubby legs. Most tortoises are small, but the giant Galapagos (ga-LOP-uh-gus) tortoise is more than 5 feet (1.5 meters) long and often weighs over 500 pounds (225 kilograms).

Turtles cannot move very fast, but their hard shells protect them from enemies. The shell is built right on the turtle's skeleton—so it can't be taken off.

The box turtle pulls its head and legs all the way into its shell. Then this turtle closes its special hinged shell so tightly that nothing can get in.

Scientists believe that turtles have existed for almost 200 million years. The turtle's protective shell is one reason that this sort of reptile has been able to survive for such a long time.

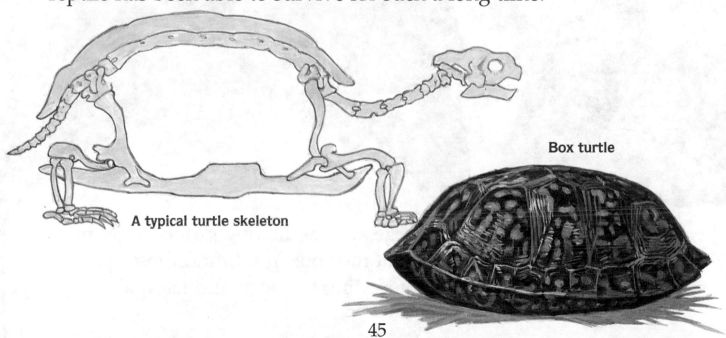

A typical turtle skeleton

Box turtle

Anole

Today's reptiles make up a large and fascinating group of animals. Try to observe them in nature or at the zoo. You'll find these special creatures and their habits are interesting to watch and learn about.